A DREAM HEAR.

A Book of Poetry and Prose of Love, Hurt, Despair, Hope, and Loneliness

Lara Phoenix

My first written words are not remembered, nor will my last ones be. Somewhere in between I hope to impart a piece of my soul onto the pages. Clean crisp paper creates a sense of urgency to fill the empty spaces. I write stories using poetry and prose. I write words of hope, love, despair, and so many other emotions. The hurt of loss and suffering pain are my pencil and pens. The white sheets and blinking curser become my lover of sorts, often arguing with me as words fail to capture the emotion.

This is the first compilation of my words.

I can only hope you will find them pleasing to your heart.

To my Mom,

I did it Momma. I miss you.

Table of Contents

Through It All

Through the beating of a heart, feel the thunder score.

Through the silence of a mind, know that trumpets roar.

Through the vision of the eyes, see the purple dying dawn.

Through the noise upon the lips, taste the bitterness of deceit.

Through the tears raining down her face, know the pain is real.

Through the dreams upon this night, hear his screams of misery.

Through a breath wish for more.

Through thine hands, steeple a prayer.

Through thine legs, bend your knees.

Through your heart, pray for peace.

Through it all...

The Storm Swirls

The storm swirls around me, ripping and tearing at my soul.

The darkness creeps across the fields of my mind.

I am on bended knees, with my arms raised to the heavens.

My tears run rivers of blood down my face.

My heart crawls away to seek shelter from the pain. I scream into the night wind.

I beg for understanding.

I fall to the tear-soaked ground before me, curling into a tiny ball of pain.

As much as you hurt me, I still have you in my heart.

I cry for what should have been.

I cry for what could have been.

I cry.

Tears

When does the pain turn to healing?
When does the dark stop being so blinding?
When do the tears no longer burn?

Lost.

I can't describe this pain other than to say I'm lost.
I'm totally lost.
I can't see for tears.
I can't hear for my screams.
I can't feel, for you took my heart with you.

Each day is supposed to be easier.
It's a lie. Each day is harder without you.
Everything I see, or hear, or touch, reminds that you are not here
anymore.

How is it even possible to take another breath?
I can't fathom how to move forward.
I fake it through the days.
Say my hello's, how are you's, see you soon.
And slap a smile across my face.

But it is all a lie.
There just under the surface is the little brown- haired girl screaming for
you.
Crying out silently as the tears roll down her soul.

I'm not brave.
I'm not anything.
I'm a shell trying to figure out how to even look at anyone.

Tears (Continued)

How do I do this? How is it even possible to try?

I cry out for you at the oddest times.
In the middle of the grocery store, while driving on the highway, when loading the dishwasher.
There you are, slammed in the forefront of my mind.

There are so many things I want to share with you.
So many things to tell you.
No use.

You can't hear me anymore.

Light Bulbs or New Love – You Decide

The old light is dark and heavy, breathing a foggy mist of disgust.
Crackles of power weakly seep from its veins.

Deep vibrations exalt its coming death.
Fractures of cold splinter its skin and sour its breath.
The last vestiges of light flickers its final goodbyes.

Springing forth from the darkness new light dances into the corners.
New light is crisp and fresh with adventure.

Molecules dance in the air for attention.
It breathes an air of purity and song.
Hearts open wide to accept colors of change.
Power surges with delight and fancy over pages of rhyme and reason.

New light delights in laughter and joy.
Finding peace only when its master is safe.
New light grows into a powerful maturity, only to metamorphosis into old light with cunning swiftness.

Old light is dark and heavy........

Forever Embedded

I see you.
The shimmering hope of light filtering down from the dark.

I feel you.
The soft edges of promise that glisten on the warm water.

I smell you.
The earthen beast of the deep forest.

I hear you.
The whispering sounds of laughter wavering amongst the branches of
the pines.

I know you.
The golden hues of promises on the tips of the clouds.

I need you.
The rhythms of a heartbeat I remember from long ago.

Touch my heart and set me free.
Sing to me and let me heal.
Speak to me so I may hear.
Unbind my wings so I may soar.
Release my lips so I may speak.

Forever embedded on the hope of tomorrow is the love we cherish in
the sunset of today.

Gone Is The Summer

My soul swims in the misery of winter.

The long dark nights swim in my heart.

The bitter cold has hardened the marrow of my bones.

The bleak sky matches my blurry vision.

How long before summer comes again?

My body is cold without your warmth.

My hands shake at the loss of you.

My tears have frozen upon my cheeks.

My mouth trembles trying to remember your touch.

How long before summer comes again?

Where is the passion that once scorched our brow?

Where is the love that once sheltered our hearts?

Where is time we once laughed away?

Where is our future?

How long before summer comes again?

Time passes with no alleviation.

My sluggish heart crawls further on.

My soul is beaten and battered.

No more tears can fall from my eyes.

Solar Eclipse

Yes, my sweet love, I have finally caught you.
I have chased you many years over many continents.
Your bright rays filling the earth below with your love and nourishment.
Your heat I remember from days long past.
I have watched your beauty dip over the crest of the western sky.
The glimpse one of wonder and awe.

The magnetic pull of my heart beats against the sandy beaches with my
tears.
The leaves fall from the trees as my ache is acute.
I whisk across the sky day and night attempting to reach you.

Now, yes now my dearest, I have caught you in my embrace.
Even if only for a moment my heavenly body covers yours.
My darkness blankets you with the all that I am.
Your light now illuminating only around the circumference of my soul.
My darkness bringing a cool breeze to the earth far beneath us.

The corona of our destiny will last only a moment in time.
Until we meet again my love, know I will follow you always.
As you dip, I will climb.
As you climb, I will dip.

Forever in the path to reach you again one day.

Before You Too Are Black

Fists of rage cover my eyes as soundless screams leave my gaping mouth.

Fingers dance into the death filled night.

Blood, cold and laughing drips from the stars.

Twinkle twinkle lovely light, be forgotten another night.

Blistered flesh drags across the meadow floor.

Toes tap to the harps broken song.

Ping ping the rain screams.

Foliage turns its head away.

Low does the willow bow when first my heart no longer beats.

Moonlight breaks upon the wind, carries to darkness its golden hue.

Swirling dances of butterfly wings crashes to hell in fiery ice.

Broken glass heals the soft edge of touch.

Kiss me lover before you too are black.

Kiss me lover before you too........ are black.

I Scream

I scream. I scream. I scream.
You do not hear me.
I whisper. I whisper. I whisper.
You do not hear me.

We are the same, yet not alike.
Once we loved each other.
Now we..... *sigh*

The pain pulls my soul from me.
My eyes bleed. My tongue is swollen.
The valves of my heart are dry.

Your talons rip at my heels. Pulling me down.
Pulling me low to the ground. The sky is dark.
with your hate. Yet I can gander a light above.

I lay wasted upon the floor. No longer able to
live this life. I have fought for you. I gave you
all I had to give. And you took it all.
You took everything I had to give.
And then you took even more.

I scream. I scream. I scream.
You do not hear me for your ears are closed.
You do not see me for your eyes are opaque.
You do not love me for your heart is frozen.

I Scream (continued)

I scream. I scream. I scream.
I give up.
I will not fight you who are my demon any more.
You have won. I lay wasted upon the floor.

Quiet overtakes me. Peaceful, blissful quiet.
Yes, I am done. Take me now.

Wait! We are here! Do you hear us?
We who are not of your blood, but who are your
family call to you.
We are here! Do you hear us?

A buzzing enters my mind. What? Who is that?
We are your family. We are here for you.
To care for you. To foster your heart.
To bolster your soul. To lift you up above the pain.
To lift you up to the clouds.

What? I know not of what you offer.
My mind is a haze of pain and disappointment.
I cannot hear you.
I am done with the pain.

Stand up Warrior.
Stand up now!
You are not done.
But just begun.
Pick up your mighty staff.
Step up to us.
We are here for you.
We will lift you up.
You must take the first step into the light.

Stand up Warrior.
Stand up now!
You are not alone.
There is much to be done.
There is work to do.
Pick up your mighty staff.
Look up.
See the light.

We are here for you.
But you must be here for yourself.

I scream. I scream. I scream.

And someone heard....

Darkness Plays At The Fringes Of My Mind

Darkness plays at the fringes of my mind.
Why has the deep-seated sadness parked in my heart I cannot say.
Maybe it is the child who cries from starvation day after day, or the man
who grieves his lost friend, or maybe the girl who has cried for days
because her lover has gone amiss.
Whatever it is, it has festered so deep in me it is consuming me. I can
barely see beyond the darkness.
Everything plays before me in blurry shadows.
There is little light around me.

I am not even sure I am me anymore.
Have I changed so vastly because of all this pain that I can't find myself
anymore?
Maybe I don't really exist.
Maybe I only exist when someone thinks of me.
Like those elusive dreams.
You know the good ones, the happy ones.
The people in them are alive only when you have the dream.
Maybe that is all I am.

Blinking my eyes trying to focus on anything of substance is to no avail.
Spider webs of influence cloud my judgement.
Whispers of memories and the musical notes of hope fade with the
waning of the day.
How is it possible that another day has passed so suddenly, yet
excruciatingly slow?
In mere moments the day flies by on wings turning quietly into
yesterday
and the fabric of tomorrow stretches in endless agony before me.

Darkness Plays At The Fringes Of My Mind
(Continued)

Blood patterns of each step I take mar the pristine white floor.
Not wanting to move forward yet caught in a tidal wave of necessity
they are stripped bare of flesh.
The tattered remnants of the silk gown lay heavily upon my weary
shoulders.
Its once brilliant green hue has dulled to gray.
Its final cry of detest is heard as it sweeps the floor falling from my
shoulders shirking its responsibility to cover me.

A far-off wail sits on the periphery of my ears.
I do not wish to hear this.
Please go away I beg and leave me to fester in the dark.
Fluttering lashes push back the tears as I lean on the windowsill.
My gnarled hands grasp the edge as I gaze out the window in search
of my heart.
I am not sure I can hear it in this condition, but I must try to or face a
certain death at the hands of this burdensome weight.

Your Voice

Your voice whispers along the freckles of my flesh.
My spirit dances naked in the rain for you.

My heart skips a beat when your eyes devour my lips.

Your arms embrace my passion with the strength of a warrior.

My soul explodes in a blazing glory from your tending loving.

Your touch feathers across my temple to easy my burden.

My breath expels in heated bliss upon the wings of night.

Together we transcend time and space into the abyss of forever.

Silent Wings

A tingling up my spine had me turning to look for the source.
I scanned the crowded room looking for anything out of place.
The tinkling of glasses and laughter mixed with the music made it
almost impossible to really hear what anyone was saying.
I was standing with two friends when I first became aware of you.
That tingling was you.
The fact that you were here was an amazement to my spirit.
Even as close as you are, I cannot find you.
Then my eyes lock onto you.
There, right there.
Only a few feet away is the liquid to my parched soul.
The rain to my desert sand.

Our eyes meet for the briefest of moments.
You nod your head and I nod in return. I close my eyes hoping it is not
a mirage.
When I open them again you are gone.
Yet I know you are real.
I can feel you inside me now.
A drizzle has begun.
A nice warm drizzle of emotion begins to fill me.
I smile as I make my way around the room speaking to one friend and
then another.
How do I rush them out of my home, so I can focus on finding you is my
only thought.

Hours later the last of my friends leave and I am finally alone.
Not bothering with cleaning, I quickly pull the curtains, lock the doors,
and
shut off the lights.
I need the quiet to bring you to me again.

Stripping off my clothes, I stand in the light of the fireplace and await your arrival.
Come to me my love.
It has been too long since your last visit to my soul.

Bathed in the light and warmth of the fireplace, I stretch my arms out parallel to my shoulders with my palms facing inward.
Holding the stance so you can see I have nothing but love in my heart.
I hold no weapons to harm you, hide no evil to bind you.
I am here naked of intention.
I need only to feel your arms around me.
To know that once again I am yours.
That I give all I am to you and only you.
In return all I ask is you to want to be mine and only mine.

There in the flickering light I begin to see you taking shape.
Coming out of the shadows you approach on silent wings.
Your body wraps closely around mine.
Together we twine our limbs to become one.
We dance the dance of love and light.
We pull and push our bodies to ecstasy's end.
Whispered promises breach our lips as we nip and nibble to our hearts content.
You consume me with your heated touch and burn the edges of my buried
soul.

As I lay deep in the crook of your arm, our hands intertwine under the dying light of the fire.
The swelling of my heart tips me over to the peace of sleep where you are always waiting.
Tears fill my eyes as I know when I awaken you will be but air upon my flesh.

Firefly
(Written on the eve of my Mother's passing)

Firefly, firefly come sit by me.
Share your tales of nights gone by.
Shine your light into this dark night.

Lighting on the arm of her chair, I speak my words only she can hear.
Oh sweet lady, what adventures I have had.
What joy and wonderment the world does hold.

Landing lightly in the palm of her hand, I am astonished that she hears
me.
I have delightful things to share and many stories to tell, if you have
a moment to spare.
There are mountains to climb, and clouds to watch; there are rivers that
flow, and stars that shine; and there are flowers to smell, and rain
to listen to.

She listens intently as I tell tales of whispers in the night, of love found
and lost, of babies' gurgles and simple pleasures.
My wings flutter as I rise from her hand to rest upon her shoulder.
The stories continue long into the night, then as my light begins to fade,
I rush to finish to the end.

Above all things I have seen and done, there is one thing I must know.
Please tell me sweet lady about the love in your heart.
Tell me quick before I must go, do you love, how does it feel? Is it pure
and is it dear?

Hearing the whispers of the bug in my ear, tears form and fall upon
my cheeks.
Oh yes, little bug, all kinds of love fill my heart.

Take all the wonders that you have seen and heard and know it won't come close to the love in my heart. The tears still flow as my breath catches quick.

My heart is full and empty too.
With love there comes pain and joy, peace and comfort.
But the love most precious of all is the love we take for granted.
The love we don't miss until it's gone.

He rises from my shoulder and buzzes around my face as his light begins to waver, I know I must end.
You see dear firefly, for all the wonders of the world, there is no wonder greater than the love from heaven.
There are mountains to climb, and clouds to watch; there are rivers that flow and stars that shine; and there are flowers to smell and rain to listen to.
Most of all, there is love to behold.

There are hands to be held, lips to be kissed, whispers to be heard, laughter to be shared.

There are tears to wipe, and anger to be cooled.
There are hearts to be mended and lives to be lived.
And then one day, there is love to be lost.
No mountain, no cloud, no star above can heal the wound of love that is lost.

The firefly begins to turn away.
Off into the night I see his light flicker low as he turns to me and whispers his final words.

Firefly (Continued)

Oh sweet lady, do you not know, that all you love is here to stay?
Whether day or night, or near or far, love never pales.
Have no fear of losing the love, it comes alive with only a thought.

So close your eyes, and think of me, for once I was your Bumble Bee.

Colors

I lay here in my cocooned bed sheltered from the world around me.
You slowly peel back the petals of my rose.
One by one they fall away.

The black of darkness.
The blue of pain.
The red of lies.
The green of anger.

You don't give up. You don't give in.

The colors of life surround us.

Sweet Destiny

The destiny of our lives is only a moment away.

In a blink of an eye the future becomes the present and the present has become the past.

Waste not a moment dwelling on what was or could have been.

For this moment should be lived with the ones in the here and now.

Breathe in the scents of life around you.

The blooming buds of love.

The heady scent of sex.

The warming air of need and desire.

Taste the flavors of the world you live.

The sweet love of your mate.

The tender care of a parent.

The salty tears of a child.

Hear the sounds of the universe, the rhythmic beating of its heart.

The sliding of flesh to flesh.

The whispers of lust in the wind.

Sweet Destiny (Continued)

Touch the petals of your life.

The texture of petting your lovers' hair long into the night.

The soft brush of skin as fingers touch your lips.

The heat of your soul as you are set on fire.

See the wonders alight in the dark.

The twinkling of the stars along the Milky Way.

The love in their eyes as you gaze in wonder.

The moonlight which shows the path in deep sighs.

Destiny.

Sweet destiny.

Don't waste a single moment of time.

Take and covert what is yours.

A Radiance To Light

A radiance to light any darkness in the universe.

A cool breeze to feather a heated brow.

A whisper of love to fill an empty heart.

Waiting arms to hold a lonely soul.

A love so endearing it fills the sky.

These are the things that come to mind when I think of you.

A light to fill my darkness.

A soft touch to sooth my heat.

A gentle song to fill my ears.

A love so endearing it fills the sky.

Twisted Sheets

Her voice

For here amongst the twisted sheets of life did d our souls become one.
I know he is there just out of reach.
My mind wanders back to those nights of my daring to pin prick his armor.
Now I may die without knowing his touch.

The blast of his anger does warm my heart.
He frees me of this prison of dirt and grime.
He holds me close without touching my body.
Yet my spirit does reach for him.
My heart will heal under his driving care.

His voice

She. Her. Mine.
She is mine and no one will dare to challenge it.
I will find her and bring her home.
Here, this earth, is my living hell without her gentle voice to calm my beast.

Yes, you are mine.
I will find you.
I have known peace but once and it was you who gifted it to me.
The beating pulse of your life I will protect.

The darkness surrounds me, but it will not consume me.
You are all I think about.
The wind of hope will guide me to you.
You forever you.

I have found you in the bowels of darkness.
You ceased the life of your tormentor.
You brought me into the light of your heart.

Their voice

Now we are together. Fire of our bodies keep our home warm.
Together. We. Us. Forever. Now we live and love. Now our family grows.
We are alive together as one.

Her Voice

To die a little death in your arms each day is my heaven on earth.
Now sweet love, now.

No Voice

Angled planes of this male lay alongside the smooth softness of her
body.
Sheets twists, bodies bowed, skin glistens. Moans of desire devoured in
kisses.
Peaked breasts, blood pumping, liquid heat of pleasure.

Passion Ride

Kisses at the hollow of my neck.

Breaths of fire along my spine.

Moans of pleasure float in the air.

Trickles of passion run down my breasts.

I climb his body to reach its peak.

And slowly glide to heavens gate.

His tongue pierces my gasping lips.

He paints my mouth with his probing tongue.

My hands gain purchase upon his shoulders.

My hair swings long across my jousting hips.

He holds my hips to keep the pace.

And dips his head to suckle my hardened peak.

The slap of skin beats a mighty rhythm.

His tongue dances to my other breast.

My fingers twine into his hair.

A tug of passion uplifts his face.

Our tongues dance a matching beat.

A crescendo of power is lit deep below.

Our eyes are locked as he takes control.

A power surge of his hips he bucks.

I tilt my hips for one last moan.

His hand scorches my tender bud.

Together we peak the crest of passion.

Our foreheads together as our breath is quicken.

A lingering kiss to scorch the night.

I climb down from my mountain peak.

And lay beside my passion beast.

He tucks me close and snuggles deep.

What Are Dreams?

Are they the nightly whispers of tomorrow's promises?

Or maybe your soul leaves your earth-bound body and lives another life.

Or perhaps it's the revisiting of what has happened in a previous life.

Does it really matter?

Will you change who you are or what you do because of a dream?

Will you forge ahead and spread your wings to fly high above the clouds.

Of course, dreams matter.

Whether it be a nightly adventure or an afternoon daydream, dreams keeps our colors bright.

Our vision is crisp.

Our music is loud.

Take hold of that dream.

Grab it by the tail.

Swirl it around the room and over your head.

Let it land at your feet.

Then take a moment to watch it change.

Add your own spices, a dash of color, a heaping of faith, and a lot of hard work.

Your dream will cry, grumble and groan.

Foster it gently, teach it how to crawl, then walk, then run.

It will mumble under its breath.

Teach it to speak, to form sentences, to have discussions.

Give it a voice.

Allow your dream to grow, to change, and metamorphose.

Allow your dream to become your daily bread.

Then live your dream.

Love your dream.

Be your dream.

Dream Lover

The warrior watches her in the dark.
Her lovely features outlined by the moonlight through the window.
His heart drums out a beat of loneliness and despair.
How he wants to love her.
Touch her.
This night was like every other night he could remember.
Watching her.
Watching over her.
What is her name?
Who is she?
Why does he crave her so?

She dreams of him at night.
She shivers as his whispers of love caress her skin.
She longs for his touch.
How she wants to love him.
Touch him.
Are you only a dream?
An apparition my soul has created?
I am lonely sweet warrior.
Come to me.
Come into my arms.

He slowly approaches her bed.
Her sleeping form so peaceful.
So beautiful.
Am I in your dream?
Or are you an apparition my soul has created?
I am lonely sweet one.
Let me come to you.
Let me into your arms.

With gentle care he pulls away the blanket that hides her body.
His soul screams for hers.
        She turns towards him in her sleep.

A sigh of pleasure escapes her lips as the blanket exposes what it has been protecting.
Her luscious form wears no other material covering her naked beauty.

I have waited so long for you warrior.
Each night I beg you to come to me.
Now is our time my love.
Our time that we can be together.
Even in her sleeping form she beckons him to her.
Her lips beg to be kissed.
To be consumed by him.
Her body arches as if he were holding her.

Her ethereal beauty stuns him.
Dare he touch her?
Would she feel it?
Would she know he is there?
His hand reaches out to smooth away a lock of hair hiding her face from him.
My God, he can touch her.
He can feel her.
I am here my sweet one.
I am finally here.
His soul weeps in joyous agony.

She moans in her sleep but does not awaken.
Her pink tongue sweeps across her lips.
An arm falls to the side of the bed as if coaxing him closer.
Come to me warrior.
In my arms there will be love.
I belong to you.

Her soul is anguished with the pain of loss.
He kneels beside the bed. Is it possible that you can hear me sweet one?
He prays that at last his journey is ending and he has found his heaven.
His whispers flutter like butterfly wings into her soul.

Her eyes open.
A small smile touches her lips.
A hand rises, and she touches his face. Finally, warrior.
Finally, you have come home to me.

Her touch is soft and pleasing.
He places his hand on top of hers.
I can feel you.
Yes, sweet one I am finally home.
He presses his lip ever so lightly upon hers. She sighs into his mouth.
Heaven awaits us my love.

He eases into bed beside her.
Holding her close.
Their hearts beat as one, their souls whispering to each other.
He touches her face, kisses her lips, whispers in her ear.
I am forever yours.

And I am forever yours my husband.
I have waited so long for you to come to me.
Take me with you back to heaven.

Looking through the window, the moon smiles and the stars breath as two souls come together again and leave this earth in a swirling mist of love and light.

See It Now

Piano notes float in waves over the sharp edges of the day.

Whistling high tones tickle the wings of the night birds.

Sinewy strums a beat of the sinking sun.

Pointed keys soften the edges of tomorrow's dream.

See it now for it is here.

See it now for it was here.

See it now for it is gone forever.

Etchings Of My Heart

My body trembles with the etchings of the words yet to be spoken.
The whisper softness of hope surrounds the aching muscle in my chest.
A heart once deflated by harsh words now pumps refreshed life into my soul.
Each night you lift me from my worries and bathe me in the delicious warmth of your arms.

I feel the scraping of your pen upon my flesh.
Your words writing a decadent tale.
Yes, please, I wish you to plunder my body with each word of a poised piston.
The burn of desire grows damp and needy between my thighs.
My breasts plump at the invitation we have yet to accept.
My lips swell with the kisses I yearn to taste.

Write me a sonnet.
A sonnet of desire and greedy need.
Take me to the place where we fall over the edge of sanity.
Our bodies pulsing against each other in the mad need of release.
Allow me to writher beneath you with words only my gasping breath can explain.

Let me write the words of riding my stead to the ends of time with a rhythm only you can understand.
My gasps will be written on the walls in the language of love and earnest demands.

Tears of glory will prickle my eyes as I reach the summit only to pour amethyst love into your deep gaze.
There I wall fall into the shelter of your arms.

The words you have etched upon my soul will sprinkle my flesh.

Where have all the days gone?

(A dedication to my nephew Andrew who left us all too soon)

The days of jumping in rain puddles.

The days of blowing bubble gum balloons.

Where have all the days gone?

The days of tickles and giggles.

The days of whispering best friends.

Where have all the days gone?

The days of dances on Daddy's shoes.

The days of Mommy's simple rules.

Where have all the days gone?

They are still here my friend.

They are in your heart closest to your soul.

Where have all the days gone?

They are still here my friend.

In your mind only a thought away.

Where have all the days gone?

They are still here my friend.

In the picture book you hold so dear.

Where have all the days gone?

They are still here my friend.

Where have all the days gone?

They are still here my friend.

I will hold your hand, so you don't lose your way.

Think of him. Remember him. Rejoice in his memory.

The days are not gone my friend.

The days are alight with his soul in heaven.

The days are not gone my friend.

His wings are spread wide with his eyes upon you.

The days are not gone my friend.

His smile is wide as he sees other loved ones.

His spirit is bright amongst the angels who adore him.

The days are not gone my friend.

The days are not gone.......

The End of Storms

A storm is ending in the western sky.

The weight of its bounty is beginning to lift.

The darkness no longer endless.

The corners of despair shredded with each drop of its tears.

The wicked wind of hurt hurling back into itself.

The crackle of belief begins its journey into my heart.

The arc of the season spreading her wishes upon the soil.

The storm soon to be a forgotten past.

There on the horizon of the east, do you see it?

The colors of the future are bright and bold. The breeze of spring lifts my spirits.

The light of a new day dawns upon my heart.

My feet tap to a lighter rhythm.

The seeds of tomorrow are firmly planted.

The aroma of laughter simmers in the air.

The sizzle of hope skims my lips as the last of the rain kisses me.

Moon Lover

With whispered wings I reach for you.

My body lies splayed open upon the soft sands of your flesh.

The hardness of your body presses urgently against mine.

Only the warmth of your embrace sooths me.

The illumination of your smile brings me to fulfillment.

I look upon your face finding comfort in knowing each curve and angle.

The man I see is unlike any other before you.

Your pull is strong, bringing me to bear time and again.

The pattern of your love is as old as time itself.

You surround me with your warm embrace, covering me with your body.

Protecting me, coveting me, loving me.

You whisper words that only lovers speak.

Words only I can hear.

I whisper them back to you, but you never hear me.

You make promises to stay yet you leave each time.

You are here, then you are gone.

Even as you leave I look for you again.

With each return I wait for your departure.

Yet here I stand waiting for you once again.

Call me Moon Lover.

Call my name and I will fall at your feet.

Call my name and I will fly through the cloudless night to reach you.

Call my name and I am yours.

Call my name.

Call my name.

Words of Love

The words of my love for you is written in Braille along the dips and valleys of my body.

The pads of your fingers read every word even while more are being etched into my flesh.

The never-ending litany of hopes and dreams twirls around my wrists and ankles binding me to you beyond reason.

Wordless breaths coast through my soul feeding my heart with each cresting crash of our bodies.

My lips grow plump as you sip along the crease with increasing urgency to plunder my mouth.

The arc of love is stronger.

The colors of life are brighter.

The musky scent of need blinds me. You call me your beacon.

I call you my everything.

You lift me up when I stumble.

I stand beside you when the darkness calls.

You are here before me.

Yet I falter in its truth.

There is a shadow amongst us.

One that lives within you.

One that feeds you.

Am I strong enough to share your heart?

Are you strong enough to protect our love?

These are the things we must attend to before it destroys us; before this most precious gift we have succumbs to the evil that waits within the words of love.

Existence

I seek you in the dark of night.

I seek you in every corner.

I beg you to make yourself known to me.

You who does not exist.

Why do you tease me within my dreams?

Why do you touch my cheek with your hand?

Why am I a fodder for your joke?

You who does not exist.

Deep in my heart I pray for you.

Deep in my soul I cry for you.

Deep in my sleep I dream for you.

You who does not exist.

Your heart does beat a pounding rhythm.

Your eyes do search within my soul.

Your breath does whisper in my ear.

You who does not exist.

Existence (Continued)

Dreams are full of your smiling face.

Dreams are alive with your cunning grace.

Dreams pull me tight into your arms

You who does not exist.

There we lay upon our bed we made.

There within our home we live.

There below our midnight sky.

You who does not exist.

Bring me home oh lover mine.

Bring me to our plane we live.

Bring me close, to calm my heart.

You who does not exist.

My eyes are weary of this dream.

My heart is heavy of the burden.

My body is weak without your love.

You who does not exist.

You touch my arm with warm caress.

You kiss my eyes with tenderness.

You whisper for me to please awaken

You who does indeed exist.

There amongst the bounded sheets.

There within my hearts delight.

There beside me evermore.

You who does indeed exist.

Your smile lights a fire within my soul.

Your eyes of blue do hold me close.

You mouth does kiss my furrowed brow.

You who does indeed exist.

My eyes are open to finally see.

My ears do hear the words you speak.

My heart expands upon your laugh.

You who does indeed exist.

You who does indeed exist.

Dream Of Me

In the dead of the night when you are alone fear not for I am here.

See me not but feel the vibrations of my heart stir the blanket upon your shoulder.

As you dream of white clouds and blue skies, I whisper words into the sandman's essence that he will guide you across time and space.

I am but a membrane of reality away.

My hand glides over your face. You feel me not.

If only you could cross the divide between our worlds.

I yearn for the acknowledgment of me in your eyes.

Somewhere in this vast universe our souls will once again meet.

There upon a midnight dream I ride my steed to higher ground. Maybe here you will see me.

Again, I try.

I sing the songs of wistful notes. Maybe now you can hear me.

I cry the tears of a woman unloved. Maybe now you can feel me.

I kiss the grapes upon which you feed. Maybe now you can taste me.

Dream of Me (Continued)

You remain untouched by my attempts.

You know not of my existence.

You are so close.

And never could you be further from me.

Yes, I am there. I am here.

I am in your dream.

Finally.

Sleep well my love. Dream your dreams of white clouds and blue skies.

Dream of a woman walking to you beside her steed, she sings songs of love, and cries tears of hope.

Eat the grapes she offers as you sit beneath the sycamore trees.

Hold her hands and kiss her lips.

Yes, my love for now your dreams are all we have.

Dream of me.

Your Light

I was but a seed until you nourished me.

I was but a dream until you held me.

I was but a tear until you smiled at me.

I was but an empty vessel until you filled me.

Your light was soft and gentle, and I grew in your warmth.

We were but strangers until I grasped your hand.

We were strong when the other was weak.

We were close and yet far apart.

We were happy when could have been sad.

Your light was bright, and I grew tall.

You gave me life and held me dear.

You watered my soul and fed my body.

You enriched my life and made me whole.

You pushed me forward and made me complete.

Your light grew dim as I became bright.

Your Light (Continued)

I am alone now you are gone.

I cry my tears to hear your voice.

I remember your smile though I no longer see you.

I long for your touch though I cannot feel you.

Your light went out and broke my heart.

Your light shines bright from within the gate.

Your light shines bright through the billowing clouds.

Your light shines bright above the ocean.

Your light shines bright on your angel wings.

Your light shines bright.

Five Stages of Loss

There are many forms of loss in life. The first loss of a pet. The first loss of a loved one. Maybe it is a loss of a job, or maybe the loss of a friendship. Or perhaps, as in my case, it is the loss of a love. Regardless of the loss, the steps to moving on are the same.

Oh, how sweet the first stage is. Denial in its wonderful void of understanding. Denying the fact that the loss occurred. Denying that it hurts as much as it does. If we do not deny then we must accept. And we are not capable of that at this point. So, we deny. We deny they are gone, that they left.

We deny the truth of each breath we must take without them. Instead, we prefer to live in our fantasy world that they only left for a moment. A quick run to the store just knowing in our heart they will walk through the door at any moment. A departure at the train station that will soon return them to our loving arms.

We wallow in the gray matter of our hearts putting up all barriers we can create to hold onto that denial. Giving up is not an option. He or she will return. The love was pure, right? You did all the right things, you gave all you had to give, so they will return. It was only a moment ago that their whispered voice was heard in your soul about their undying love and devotion.

The protective wall of denial holds back reality until we can handle reality. Somewhere in the darkness, the icky bit of denial begins to ease its way along the nerves. The reality stings no matter the amount of denial we try for force into our brains. It simmers and boils until the top blows and anger smiles its evil toothless grin as it takes over. Anger is quite striking in the beauty of loss. For all the denial that we have, anger kills the denial in one swift stab to the heart.

Anger strikes out with a vast swing covering all of those around us. Anger is a sweet treat after the cloudy trip of denial. While angry we question many things about the relationship. Why did you do this or that? Why did they do this or that? Why did this happen? How could you have stopped it? What more could you have done? Why weren't you enough? Why wasn't there an option to save the relationship? Why? Why? Why? We question everything we did or did not do.

We question the values you once had. We even question if any of the professed love is worth all this pain. We stomp our shattered heart on the doorstep of anger in the hope that somehow it will begin to make sense. If the person who we lost were in front of us, we would not know whether to pull them close in great jubilation or kill them on the spot for all the hurt they caused you.

And with that very thought, we begin to bargain. We bargain with ourselves on how to be better, do better, say better…. We bargain with whatever deity we believe in to give you another chance to make it right. We make speeches in front of the mirror, practicing our facial expressions and body language on what we would say and how we would look if we only got that one more chance to convince our lost love that you are the one and only one for them.

We belittle ourselves in the process, yet we do not care. All we can think of is what it was like when things we good. You know, really good. The laughter, the jokes, the midnight talks, the good mornings, and teasing texts, the nicknames that made you giddy. Oh please, let us have that one more time. I will make it right, we will make it right. I will change, I will be different, tell me what it is you need me to do and I will do it.

What a blooming fool. For at this point we are beginning to understand there is no going back. There is no chance, there never was. Nodding your head in clarity of what has been lost, the anger that has passed, and that bargaining is out of the question, we move into true and deep depression.

Depression flows freely through every synapse in our brain. Our heart stutters and our lungs burn with each breath. Sadness becomes the mantra of our life. We move like zombies as all else is hidden from us except this black well of despair. Oceanic waves of tears threaten to drown us as we gasp for air.

Daily functions become obsolete as caring about living is so far from your mind all you want to do is pull the covers over your head and pray another day will slip by. Thoughts are muddled as family and friends try to help.

All you want to do is to be left alone in your own misery. The levels of depression are so high and low you become dizzy with the effects of trying to keep your sanity.

Memories of the past waver in your mind bringing you great joy, only to be shattered on the cliffs of reality. Nothing will ever be the same. What I find so bizarre about this stage is that the highs are super high. So high I can soar to the stars with a full heart for what we had, in the next moment the low is devastatingly debilitating to the point I am on my knees.

I have stayed in this stage a long time. Not able to go back or move forward. Not sure I know how. They say this is hardest step to move out of. I believe it. I so believe it. I have days of laughter of sorts.

I have days I can hold regular conversations and the memory of us slips into a quiet corner giving me peace. I even have days I think, that maybe, just maybe, I can function along with everyone else. Then low and behold some small word, or action, brings it back to me full force.

Slamming once again into the frontal lobe of my brain and I fall into a heaping pile of misery.

Where oh where is acceptance? I deserve this level of grief. I deserve to be free of the purest pain imaginable. I deserve to be able to live again. Don't I? So where is it? Why have I not gained this level? Am I still not worthy of the freedom it would bring?

Oh wait! I think I have it.

My acceptance is this…… Love is bad.

I finally get it.
Love is not worth having.
Love is a lie.
Love sucks.
Love is for fools.
Love is bad.

Reflections In Your Dreams

The whispering songs of lovers riding along the night breezes.

The hope of tomorrow's promise are the goose bumps on your arm.

The cool breath of the moon upon your shoulder.

Where are you my love, the waves ask.

Where are you?

Turn around dear one, for I am here.

Look for me among the darkest of nights.

Close your eyes and seek me for I am here.

Close your eyes and come to me my love.

I am here, a reflection in your dreams.

Today

What tomorrow brings is only a guess.

Only a whisper of thought, only a grain of sand.

Today is what we have in front of us.

Do with it as you will.

Fight it.

Love it.

Hate it.

Do it.

Whatever "it" is.

When the dawn of today arrives remember that tomorrow is still tomorrow.

Today never changes its name to yesterday or tomorrow.

Those are her sisters used for regrets and wishes.

It is beyond our ability to change yesterday or foresee the tomorrow.

Wisely be kind to today, for she is your only reality.

She has great power and is unforgiving in her relentless pursuit to keep you forever in her grasp.

Today (Continued)

Today will not move over for yesterday or tomorrow.

She is steadfast in her stance over the here and now.

She stands proud at the peak of our world. Using her strength to keep us moving to and fro like magnets to steel.

Stand tall with passion in your today.

Be loud about who you are and what you do.

Be proud of your ability to forage through her jungle for your slice of life.

Remember today is your only reality.

Today will never give up on you.

Today will be here as long as you need her.

Today is always today.

Autumn

Oh, where will you take me my old friend?

What secrets do you hide around each bend?

What tales of the past would you share?

And what adventures would I find there?

Autumn gives me a small laugh at my audacious questions.

Take my path he says, and I will show you many wonders.

I will teach you about life and dreams and hope.

I will lead you to new engagements for your soul.

Take up a staff to lean upon when you tire.

For this is a never-ending journey.

Come with me if you so dare.

His laughter was light and floated upon the wind.

His caress upon my brow was like an angels' wings.

I picked up a mighty staff to begin my journey.

The branches ebbed and flowed with the breeze, beckoning me to quicken my gait.

Music of the season filled the crisp cool air.

The sunlight danced amongst the trees.

Autumn (Continued)

I could not hasten my step.

For there was much to behold with every step I did make.

I could hear his voice ring clear as he shared his home with me.

There upon the grass, do you see, the sweet kiss of morning dew is still alive.

Harken your ears, do you hear, the water from the creek is singing a glad song.

Pick up that leaf, do you feel, the veins of life throbbing within.

Breathe deep, do you smell the earth opens her heart with a sensual bouquet?

As I turn the next bend to my eyes delight I find a small field of flowers with petals reaching for the suns kiss.

Alas, he says, it is their final days.

It is time for them to return to earth and replenish their spirit.

Come further down the path for there is more to see.

The tree over here, she has small saplings nearby.

And here on my side, do you see, the family of rabbits sharing a meal.

Over here is the mighty Oak who bears the name of many lovers.

Autumn (Continued)

Shhhh, be still now, and you will hear the cry of Summer as she goes to sleep.

Yet in her place, there just around the next bend of your journey, listen close, you can hear the beginnings of the chorus of our sweet Autumn.

Just a slight murmuring of notes. Clear and crisp does our Autumn sing.

I listen close, and yes, I can hear the tinkling of music like crystal bells.

I continue my journey with my heart open wide.

Taking in the wonders he chose to provide.

More wonders with each step.

Memories of those who had taken this journey before me.

As I near the end of the path he speaks to me one last time.

Here before you is a path many have traveled.

But few have taken the time to see.

I shared my life with you, so you might bring others to see.

We are lonely for the company and laughter of your kind.

Come back often to walk my path again, and I will share new wonders each time.

We offer you kindness, hope and dreams.

You have only to take a step.

Autumn (Continued)

Before you now is another path.

I hope you will move forward and remember each day is a journey.

All you have to do is take the first step.

As I looked up, I saw the path had ended.

He was quiet once again.

Looking back, I saw his wave of goodbye through the branches dancing to the tune of the wind.

Goodbye my friend. I will return soon, and I will bring others with me.

The path was filled with many delights.

My mind was clear.

My heart was light.

And Autumn filled my soul.

Forget Me Not......

Were you a figment of my heart's imagination?
Did you ever really exist?
Maybe you were only meant to be a whisper of hope.
Something to keep me going century upon century.
The loss of you is more than I care to acknowledge.
I mean, I cannot call it a loss since I never had you.
I can only miss what I had hoped we would have.

That's it, isn't it?
You were only a hope.
A voice in the night created by a desire to be loved.
Your voice, your cries, your need of me, built up in my mind to be more
than it could ever be.
Right?

The scent of you in my nostrils a lie of hunger I fed upon.
The soft touch of your hand on mine, now crushing my dream of being
in your arms.
The sound of your voice when you whispered in the night, now a
howling memory.

These are the lies I tell myself night after night without a sign of you.
No voice calling to me, no words to kiss my ears.
No vision of you next to me to nourish my eyes.
No warmth from that ever so brief touch of you to burn my desire.

Moonlight Away

To hear the ocean in your heart does not make it empty.

It makes it full of hope and yearning.

The never- ending pursuit of the waves to reach the embrace of the shore before crashing on the jagged edges of reality mimics the beat of our heart.

It is hope that keeps the lungs expanding and exhaling each minute.

The inhale of the next moment is when the future of which you were destined begins to unfurl before your eyes.

The circle around the moon is the hazy light of which to wish upon.

For the one you seek is wishing upon it too.

Out there in the tomorrows not yet created is the one for you.

She or he too, lay their head upon the feathers to dream of a love such as you seek.

There is someone.

The moon knows this.

That is why his light still shines upon you.

I hope you find your one…. The one. We all seek it.

We rejoice in seeing others find it.

Yet those of us alone stumble and falter looking at the moon hoping ours is but a moonlight away.

Harvest For The Soul

Spider webs rise and fall with the gentle breeze.
Yellow dying leaves fight their swirling death to the moist ground.
The hummingbirds no longer suckle from their nectar.
The light of day slips under the horizon a little quicker.
Morning is slower to find its warmth from the sun.
The call of the loon is louder as it searches for a mate.

These are the thoughts that crossed my mind today.
Sitting on the porch allowing the change of the season to enter my soul.
To stir within my cobwebbed mind that no matter these things that I
see, feel, and touch, there is much more to this change.

An awakening of my essence if you will, so allow me to share.
Today as the warmth of the sun was slight, I embraced her even more.
I opened myself to her love and care she pores upon us each day.

The dying of the leaves screamed at me to not forsake the coming of
their death.
But to rejoice in their death.
To bear witness to all the shade and kindness from the heat they have
provided, and to allow them their shining moment as they change
colors.
This is their screaming against their death.
From green, to pale yellow, to orange and red and deepest purple.

They scream their life and death at us.
Do not forget what they have provided.
And remember in their death they replenish the earth with their
nourishment for springs eternal birth.

Harvest For the Soul (Continued)

The gentle breeze whispers to me of the coming coolness in the days ahead.
The wind chimes come alive under his caressing touch.
Flags fly with grandeur of attention as he lifts their life story for all to see.
He brushes against my legs bringing chilled bumps to the surface.
As he blows his breath through the trees, the birds still sing a mighty song.
One of hope, of love, and of pain.

Their days of lighting upon the windowsill will be narrow as they try to stay warm, as they nestle together in their little homes.
As I opened my window this morning he kissed my brow reminding me to harken my body with blankets as the chill entered my bones.

The sun was bright this day, bringing with her a semblance of warmth.
She worked hard this day to keep her fire stoked.
But alas, she is weakened from her summer toils.
Her biting heat only a memory.
Today she offered what she had, a pure warmth to open the mind and cleanse the cobwebs in my soul.
She now begins her decent over the horizon.
Hanging on to the edges with her shafts of light.
She gently whispers a good night with promises of tomorrow.

Harvest For The Soul (Continued)

Sitting here on my porch this day, I was graced with a warm sun, a gentle breeze, birds singing their songs, and a wind chime playing their tune.

I watched with wonder as leaves disengaged themselves from their mother tree.

They swirl in a kaleidoscope of color making their journey to the earth. At times a breeze would pick them up, lifting them up higher than they had ever been before, and then releasing them, so they could finally alight upon the ground to take their last breath upon their resting place.

Taking a deep breath, I opened my soul to the day.

I heard the fluttering of birds' wings, listened to a felines purr at my feet.

I felt the love of the sun upon the earth, embraced the kisses of the breeze upon my body as the harvest of the season filled my soul.

What Tomorrow Brings

Storms chasing through the night sky seeking a place of haven.

Winds pushing its own agenda to bring the cooler breeze.

Music and laughter singing in the crisp air warming the soul.

Smiles and hugs lifting our spirits as time moves swiftly by.

Whispers of secrets, giggles of delight and hugs being shared.

Bright smiling faces bring a peace to broken hearts.

Love is abounding on the scented breeze of the night air.

Seagulls streaming by, their wings beating a pattern of freedom envied.

Clouds happily dance by, waving goodbye to today.

Blue skies peeking through the trees warming our path.

The sun takes a bow as it dips over the horizon, winking at her lover moon as he crawls onto the sky.

Rhythms of the universe come together like pieces of a puzzle.

Bonds have been formed that no wind will tear apart.

What today brought is forever gone.

What tomorrow brings is for us to forge.

Forever

Your voice whispers along the freckles of my flesh.

My spirit dances naked in the rain for you.

My heart skips a beat when your eyes devour my lips.

Your arms embrace my passion with the strength of a warrior.

My soul explodes in blazing glory from your tender loving.

Your touch feathers across my temple to ease my burden.

My breath expels in heated bliss upon the wings of night

Together we transcend time and space into the abyss of forever.

I Wait For You

The rain pours down upon my uplifted face.
I feel the trickling drops seep between the buttons of my blouse.
The cool wetness of each drop relieves the heated weight of my breasts.

Taking a heaving breath, the fragrant air cleanses my lungs and lifts the
fog of my mind.
Your image impresses upon my minds eyes.
Oh, what a glorious site.
The muscles of your body bulge against the confines of your uniform.

Another deep breath and you become clearer in my mind.
Your dark hair is damp from the rain.
My hand reaches up and brushes the hair from your face.
My palm caresses your cheek.
The sharp edges and planes easily sculpted with my fingers.

I step closer and feel your arms surround me.
My breasts are taut with desire.
My breath becomes labored as my desire clenches my lungs.
The rain pounds against me as the sky lashes out against the dark skies
with streaks of electric tongues.
Thunder booms across the land, shaking the boughs of rain laden tree
branches.

You whisper words only my soul can hear.
They reverberate across the synapsis of time.
Tick. Tock.

You pull me tight to your body.
Your desire presses against me.
I feel the pulses of your need.
A groan of pain breaks the quiet of our love.

I lick the rain from your lips.
Swirling my tongue across the seam.
Begging for entrance.

A clashing tango of tongue and lips.
Our throbbing dance of tongues matches the tempo of our hips.
Your hand entangles in my hair pulling back my head.

A plundering ravaging crescendo of exploration leaves us breathless yet
yearning for more.
A gentle smile breaks upon my face.

Oh, my glorious warrior.
Your battles take you far from me on many a night.
Oh, the wicked things we could do if you were but here.
I look to the sky to accept the pouring rain, knowing you are out there
fighting the freedom battle.

No rain on this night even though my cheeks are moistened, and my
breasts are cool.
Rain is not the source.

I Wait For You (Continued)

Tears. Tears created the rain on my face.
Tears cooled my breast.

The pain of missing you caused the thunder to roll and the sky to shriek
in tongs of angry fingers.
I turn away from the tears. I turn away from the pain.

Standing tall in my soul, I wait for you.
I wait for you.

Wave Soldiers

Waves of the ocean came crashing onto the shore like little tin soldiers with no thought of their own.

Pounding their boots into the sand.

Wave after wave.

Soldier after soldier.

Driven by the moons desire, they forced themselves to an agonizing death along the jagged torn rocks.

Their endless screams were at one time a beautiful melody being played to a child.

Now at the height the storm their screams could be felt in the core of your soul.

Screaming for mercy.

Screaming for love.

Little by little the waves slowed.

The soldiers no longer at the mercy of their master.

No longer beating a path to their ultimate destruction.

They began to pull back, ease away from the shore and their screams returned to that gentle and soothing song of peace and tranquility.

Tumbleweeds

Into the tumbleweeds I roll losing thought with a mindless soul.

Tomorrow's journey is yet untold.

Today I fight to breathe through the dust of yesterday.

Windswept memories crease my brow.

Goose bumps tickle as the memory of touch blisters my heart.

Yesterday's memories…. that's all they are.

Today is already gone, tomorrow never more.

My eyes bleed red.

My heart a fractured organ.

Rolling on the tumbleweeds my destiny is yet revealed.

Swish Swoosh

Swish swoosh, the sound beats around the room.
Voices whisper, pinging against each other.
Different conversations mix and mingle.

Quiet laughter, cups raised in unison, wishes passed around.
Smiles.
Hugs.
Greetings abound.

It is almost the end.
A new beginning peeks over the horizon.
Tomorrow promises what we cannot begin to comprehend.
Yesterday delivery is only a memory.
A new beginning is before us.

Take it not for granted.
Embrace every joy, heartache, and experience you are granted.
Strive to live more.
Live harder.
Live faster.
Live more of everything.
Live for all.

Swish swoosh, the sound beats around the room.

Not a party.

Not a gathering.

It is the sound of your own heart, pumping life into your soul.

Colors Of Life

The blistering yellow of hope.
The bright blues of faith.
The deep purple of passion.
The vast blackness of hurt.

We all have them.
We all live them.
What we do with them is our choice.

How we love is our destiny.
How we treat each other is our legacy.
Moving through the obstacles and challenges of life can be daunting.

It can in fact be crippling.
There lies the crux.
We see the colors, we feel the colors, yet we hesitate to grab them.
We hold back knowing our lift is fleeting.

Take hold. Grab on.
Look into your heart for the colors.
Seek them in every star, every wavering smile, every giggle, every breath.
Never let there be regret in your actions to live.
Live with faith, hope, integrity, love, and passion.

Colors Of Life (Continued)

Let not this day or the next pass by without giving console to the gifts given and yet to be received.

Be passionate in your vocation.
Be loving in your embrace.
Be kind with your words.
Be truthful in your faith.

All else will coalesce into the most beautiful rainbow of life.
More colors than you can imagine.

All the colors of heaven will be bestowed if you only believe in the colors of life.

Purple Love

Your smile warms me more than the heat of the sun.

The twinkle in your eyes is better than glitter in the wind.

The melodic sound of your voice would make Beethoven cry.

The love you give to me is a gift from heaven.

You make me a better version of myself.

You inspire me to be more than I thought possible.

You lift me up above the highest mountain.

You opened my eyes to the possibilities of life.

Our future is full of promise because of you.

Our destiny is written in our hearts.

Our tomorrows are entwined together.

Our forever is only beginning.

I am in love with you.

I am in love with your heart, your soul, your warmth.

I am in love with the way you love life.

I am in love with the love you so freely give to others.

Purple Love (Continued)

My heart is full of you.

My heart is so full, it has doubled.

My heart is so full, it beats a rhythm of your name.

My heart is so full, it beats purple love.

Night Vision

There you are.

My sweet love come to visit me once again.

Your eyes piercing the dark veil of night.

The coarse pad of your fingertips blazing a trail along my collarbone.

Soft sighs of strumming memories pulse between us.

The rustle of sheets sound as we twist in binding melody.

Each angle of your body covets and protects my rounded curves.

The darkest of night cannot keep our gaze shielded.

Here in the midst of emptiness, we find each other again.

The purity of emotion enslaving us forever within the chambers of our joined hearts.

Tumbling together into the vastness of hopes and dreams.

There we wallow in the fantasy of tomorrow.

Touch me lover.

Silken my soul only to you.

Take my hand. Lead me where else I would not follow.

Night Vision (Continued)

Kiss my lips.

Taste what waits for you.

Hold my heart.

For only you have the key.

You are the darkness to my light.

I am the light to your darkness.

Together the kaleidoscope of life lay before us.

Whispered sonnets tell our story.

The sweet notes bear witness to what we create together.

No masterful painter, nor musical composer, could create the beauty of our union.

The crashing waves upon the beach pales to the charge of your voice.

The stars in all the galaxies compare not to the lights of love shining from our eyes.

The soft sheen of rain does little to cool our heated flesh.

There you are.

My sweet love come to visit me once again.

You know we cannot be parted for long.

Our souls would wither and cease.

Reach for my hand.

Never let go.

Hold tight as we journey through the skies and kiss the stars as our laughter brings smiles to the heaven.

With Each Step

With each step I take, the wind slaps with laughter at my face.

The air in my nostrils sting with vibrant fire.

My feet are bloody and torn from the briars greedily snapping at them as I push forward.

The very ground I walk on snarls and pukes insects out of its depths to crawl upon my flesh.

The moon that once nourished my body tsks at me as it turns away.

The blood that once filled my soul leaves me dehydrated and demented.

I am torn and bleeding.

I am hungry and thirsty.

I am alone and empty.

The sun will rise again on the morrow.

With it will come hope and promise.

I stay a hand across my face, keeping my vision steady on my path.

I scorn the wind its stinging touch.

I breathe new air fragrant full of lavender.

I stomp the briars under my mighty feet.

With Each Step (Continued)

I poison my flesh against the teeth of despairing insects.

I lasso the moon and turn its face to mine once again.

The blood of life hydrates my soul and clears my mind.

I stand still for a moment to hear the universe sing a song of redemption.

My time is before me.

Nary a moment is ever to return.

I must push forward for there is never going back.

I am still torn and bleeding.

I am still hungry and thirsty.

I am still alone.

But I am no longer empty.

There is one out there made for me as I am for him.

We will dance amongst the stars.

We will burn our souls with scorching desire.

We will thrive on the challenge of discovery.

We will be relentless in our pursuit of new and exciting adventures.

With each step I take, the wind pushes me closer to you.

Time Slips Away

Time. Time slips away from us in those loud clicks of the second hand.
Tick tock goes our life.
Pain, hurt, laughter, love, life, death, all captured by the tiny pebbles of
sand that wash upon the beach.

Look closely at the sand and you will see the different shapes and colors
and microscopic life forces trying to leach out their day.
So much like us.
Our lives are filled with all these things and so much more if we were
but to try.
We are nothing more than ships in a bottle.

Our boundaries are set by our imagination.
If we have none and aren't willing to explore the world around us, we
might as well stay in the bottle.

If, however, you have the will, the desire, to see beyond the tick tock of
life, break free of your bottle.
Let your sails fully open. Let the wind of the heavens blow kisses on
your sails and take you wherever your imagination allows.

I am flying free of the bottle.
And oh, what a wonderful universe it is.
The skies are purple with passion.
The sun warms my flesh with love.
The wind kisses my brow with promise.
Today is your day.
Stay in the bottle or come fly with me.

Sometimes Quiet Is Violent

Sometimes, quiet is violent.
I hear the ticking of life as it clicks its insistent beat towards nothing.
The movement of the wind stills my soul.
I weep with need and want.
I scream silently with anger.
The pounding rhythm of life calls to me to live again.
I whisper into the realm of yesterday begging for freedom... Quietly.

Sometimes, quiet is violent.
Knowledge of the ages flips the pages, slicing my fingers on its edges.
Pulsing light begs to strike out with crackling spears of righteousness.
Harmonic symbols of love nestle deep inside thunderstorms of anger.
I hear the words as whispers in the night.
I fight against them.
I rage against them... Quietly.

Sometimes, quiet is violent.
Somber voices have begun their march on my soul.
Covering my ears, I still hear them.
Tears, oh tears upon tears have I shed until the rain soaks the earth.
My knees are stained black and blue from begging for understanding.
Out of tune piano chords play to the stars and moon matching the song
of you in my heart... Quietly.

Sometimes, quiet is violent.
If my veins were opened would the love for you bleed out?
Would I feel the cut?
Would the blade go deep enough?
Can I cut you out and still breathe?
Would I feel the release I desperately seek?
Fog of hurt and lost love let me be free of you... Quietly

Once upon a time, I smiled.
Once upon a time, I danced.
Once upon a time, I loved.
Once upon a time, I was yours.
Once upon a time...

These words flow over me as I sit on the windowsill of my bedroom.
It has been long enough.
Long enough for him to find me again.
Long enough for me to realize what I believed was yet another untruth.
It is time I step away from yesterday and see what tomorrow's sunrise will bring.
For tonight, I will seek hope in my dreams.
I am bent but not broken as sometimes quiet is violent.

The Hope Of Tomorrow

My eyes are upon the hope of tomorrow.

The dreams of my soul spring forth in visions of whispered breaths and scorching touches.

For all that I am, I yearn for more.

Heated passion rises along the silkiness of my flesh.

Perspiration runs a trickling river down my spine.

Cool cotton brushes the tender buds of my breasts.

The heels of my feet are buried deep in the soft threads of the blanket beneath me.

I gasp a growl as I awaken from my slumber with my eyes darting about the room searching for you.

The curtain over the window billows as a cool breeze greets my heated body.

My hand is shaky as it pushes long locks of hair from my face.

My eyes close for a moment to accept the truth that beats within the rhythm of the night.

Shaking my lowered head in denial, my hands grasp the edge of the bed before I rise making my way to the window.

You.

You, whoever you are, are not here with me.

I am still alone in this world.

Fighting to find you.

Fighting to stay grounded as I hear your screams.

Why do you fight me so?

What pain and suffering are you enduring but not allowing me to share?

Sliding the gown from my shoulders it slides from my body, pooling silently at my feet.

Taking a step forward I leave it and you behind me as I glide through my dream to take perch upon a cloud.

I can no longer stand to sleep in my bed.

Not again until I find you.

Not again.

Cleanse Me

Evil is at play in my mind.

Twisting and turning the wheels of fate.

Frothing at the mouth to take over what's mine.

Nae' you evil beast. Stay your distance from me.

Er' I stab you with my steely blade.

And roast you over your own pit fire.

Laughter fills the room.

The walls shake in defiance.

The floor bucks and bows as I maintain my balance.

You will not win the battle within me.

I am free of your judgement and censure.

I hurt no one with mine affections.

I stand strong within my soul.

Shrivel down to a speck of dust you evil pest.

Let the wind pick up your trailing's and disperse them up in the clouds.

The clouds shall release their rain of faith.

Cleansing me and the earth below.

*An explanation for this one is required. When reading books, we bring the characters to life. We give them the power to influence us. We offer our time and effort into reading their story. One book of which I will keep to myself, had me quite enamored with the hero. It dawned on me that unless I read that book, he doesn't exist. So this is a nod to all the heroes of all the books we read. .....*You do exist even if only in my mind.

Tears flowed from my mind.
There would be no tomorrow.
My heart was bereft.
My mind drifted into the darkness of loneliness.
I could not go on.
Not one more day.
Not one more breath.
I begged my heart to stop beating.
Why must you defy me you withered mass of hopelessness.

I am that I am.
Why must you keep my feet shackled in this earth-bound body.
I beg of you to let me go. Let my wings spread so that I may soar across the fields.

I gingerly step into the air so light upon my soul.
Looking down upon the wetlands.
Seeing the mountains from above as I alight upon a cloud.
I soar further out to sea.

Watch the whales flap their tails at me.
Oh you silly thing you cannot hope to gain freedom in the skies.
I am disdained by their exclamations and leave them behind to wallow in their simplicity.

I gain land once again.
Only to be harkened upon the cliffs of Ireland.
The mists wash away my tears.
The greens of the fields fill my heart with gladness.
The songs are fragrant with lilting tongues.
Yet this land is empty of what I need.
Again, I must go.

Maybe here or there I will find peace.
I search the hills and the valleys.
I search the caves of Greece.
The old ones whisper their tales of Gods and gold and lovers unknown.
Yet again I must go.

Maybe here in the deep rain forest between the tropics of Cancer and
Capricorn.
Where the air is laden with nurturing life.
The leaves and trees speak not of what I know.
Yet again I must go.

Ah, the desert.
The desert with its pristine sands and winds.
Maybe here is the peace I search for.
No.
The winds whip a furious tale that strips the soul.
Yet again I must go.

The rainbow arcs so high.
Its bright colors beckon me close.
At its end a pot of gold I can trade for my quarry.
The color fades before the end can be reached.
Once again, I must go.

My wings flutter under the burden of my pain.
I clatter to earth and tumble in the grass.
Sitting amidst the Gloriosa Daisy and Evening Primrose, I lay back.
Stretching my worn body in the bed of their of fragrance they cover me.

I awaken to the sound of voices.
Multitude of voices.
Their sounds daring upon the winds to reach me
Crisp voices.
Quiet mumblings.
Sing song murmurs.
Oh what is this place that whispers of love, and death.
Of color and scents.
Of lovers in the night.
Of a baby's desperate cries.
Of sights and sounds I know not of.

Pushing myself to reach this place.
Pushing myself to escape the confines of my scented bed.
My arms reaching out.
Begging for entrance.
The doors swing open.
Welcoming voices I can hear.

Children laughing.
The clinking of utensils as a meal is being devoured.
They smile at me. Gesturing me to come further into the room.
Offering me to partake of their generosity.
He stands in the corner watching me enter.
I can feel his breath upon my soul.
He beckons me closer with nary a word.

Their lives are mine if I so have a mind to take.
Their family is odd with its tinker toy soldiers.
Their music is odd as it fits not their origin.
Their love is pure but not of blood.

Between The Pages Of A Book (Continued)

Why have you brought me here I hasten my query?
My eyes upon the one who stands furthest away.
A male so delightful in vision tells a tale of a wandering warrior.
A warrior who travels not where they could.
A warrior so strong of mind it brings others to life.

I look upon another who sings with his soul.
He spins his song to make this tale more.
Yet another one enters whose eyes are aglow.
His words are not spoken.
His meaning is yet clear.
He leads me to the one in the shadows.

Yet as I turn away from the Master of the House and his mate,
one more doth enter and kneel at my feet.
This one is different from all the rest.
These eyes I know.
This smile is familiar.

This face is of mine own.
I have made a long journey to be here.
A journey many are not willing to make. He waits for me.
The one in the corner.
I stand tall and true of mine heart.
My steps are sure and quick.

As I approach him, he smiles.
A gentle smile.
Yet his eyes are sad.
So broken is his heart.
He takes my hands in his.
Turns them over.
Lays a kiss upon my palms.
So gentle they felt like a whisper.

He leans towards me.
I feel his very breath upon my face.
His body is warm.
His scent is decadent.
His hand caresses my jaw.
He whispers in my ear.

"I have waited so long for you.
Only you can give me life.
I am nothing without you.
There is no substance without you."

I reach for him.
His spine is straight and firm in my hand.
The breadth and width of him takes away my breath.
The color of his essence sweeps through my eyes.
As I reach to touch his face my mind is swirling in delight at the
adventures we shall share.
My heart swells at the love we will find between the sheets.

Finally.
I have found you.
You were here all this time.
Waiting for me.
As I walk to the bed to lay down with my hero, my breathing slows, my
heart beats a healthy rhythm.
My eyes are moist, my hands are shaking.
My fever has broken.

I open the pages of my favorite book.
My love takes me away once again.
We live. We laugh.
We love between the pages of his book.

One Last Thing

Thank you for taking the time to read my book. If you enjoyed it, I would be grateful if you would leave a short comment on Amazon. I read each one and am appreciative for your support and feedback. Your support really makes a difference and will help to make the next book better.